# BARLEY

---

*Memories of a Trail Dog*

**The story of a dog's adventures in the mountains of the New MexicoWilderness.**

**By Lance M. Huff**

Illustrated by Rexanne Jones

DIAMOND MEDIA PRESS CO.
1-304-460-1427
https://www.diamondmediapressco.com/

Copyright © 2023

By **Lance M. Huff**
All rights reserved.



**ISBN Paperback: 978-1-954368-90-3**

# Introduction

When the white man first came to the area now known as New Mexico, they found some of the most beautiful country in the world. The Indians living there had enjoyed and respected the land for centuries. Located between Arizona and Texas, and stretching along the Western side of the State of New Mexico, almost the full length of the state, it was a vast and wonderful area.

In the early 1900s men like Aldo Leopold, Ben Lilly and J. Stokley Ligon, were early to recognize the ecology of the area and all it had to offer. In_September, 1924, the first Wilderness Area, located in New Mexico, was established by The United States Government, under President Calvin Coolidge, who declared the entire area both a Wilderness and a Primitive Area. As part of the Wilderness designation, all means of motorized transportation, such as cars, trucks, four-wheelers, and so on were banned. All traffic, regardless of the purpose or cause, was to be by primitive means, such as horseback, pack animals and wagons and horses or teams. This has lead to a unique lifestyle for those who travel the Wilderness, and guide others into the area to experience the wonders found there. These special folks bring their specialized and old fashioned skills, along with saddle horses, pack mules, horses and burros, camping gear and the knowledge of how to use it all correctly, the concern for the care and keeping of the Wilderness area as intended and responsibility for the land. And it also includes the special kind of dogs that are part of this great lifestyle.

This is the story of one such Wilderness Trail Dog, Barley, as told by Barley himself.

## <u>**Chapter One**</u>:

*Barley meets Big Guy*

Hi, there, nice to see ya! My name is "Barley".… By the way, I'm retired now but I used to be a Trail Dog and worked with Creel Canyon Outfitters in the Gila Wilderness in New Mexico.

The Wilderness is a vast amount of land set in the mountains with lots of creeks, rivers, tall pines and lakes. It is so beautiful I don't even know any words to tell you about it. It is my very favorite place in all the world. Tall Folks refer to it as "pristine". I'm not exactly sure what that means but it is something like perfect. I'll accept that because Tall Folks usually know stuff like what words mean. After all, they make noise they call "talking" all the time. I've learned to understand a lot of it over the years. The dog way, that's my way, has always seemed better. My Tall Person, (I call him Big Guy) talks to me with all those soft sounds and I tell him in dog how much I love him too. Seems to work for us.

Anyway, the special thing about the wilderness is that no one is allowed to live there full time. No roads, no motorized vehicles of any kind allowed. If a person has to travel in and out, he has to do it on horse or mule back or on foot. No exceptions - none. So the Wilderness will stay beautiful and "pristine" for generations to come. I sure hope you get to see it for yourself. And if you do get to see it, remember Ol' Barley told you about it. Yep, those were the days. But I didn't always have it so good. I didn't even have Big Guy at first.

When I was a little puppy, I lived with a family who had some kids. Sometimes they played ball with me. Sometimes I could run along beside the Tall Persons' four wheeler when he went hunting for rabbits. I really did love those days. Of course, we could not go into the Wilderness with that four wheeler. So at that time I had no idea what I was missing. And the rest of the time, I spent locked up in the kennel. I really did not like that jail. To make matters worse, they locked me in there with two other dogs, bigger dogs and bullies to boot. One was a black lab and the other was an English bulldog Mastiff. The lab would pee on the water dish all day long so I had no fresh water. The Mastiff kept biting and chewing on me like I was a chew toy. It was very frustrating. I hoped something would change for me. "You've just got to keep faith," I would tell my-self. Something would have to change for me and before I knew it, that change had arrived. The time had come when a tall person came there to give me a good home.

I was really scared at first. I didn't know what to expect. That is always scarier than reality, when you don't know what to expect. He was Tall Folks and he seemed to be kind. He had a nice voice and I enjoyed hearing it. We had long walks together while getting to know each other. I call him Big Guy, because he is taller than most others.

It seems my new friend, Big Guy, had some things in his past that he needed to talk about and he shared them with me.

I was not his first dog. His first dog had been half wolf. Yep, you heard that right. Real wolf. One half timber wolf and one half Akita. I've seen pictures. He must have been amazing. Big Guy still misses him, even now. His name was "Tomb Stone" and sometimes they called him "Wolfie". I was very proud to be offered a job filling those paw tracks.

## Chapter Two :
### *In The Beginning......*

Oh, I'm sorry. I didn't properly introduce myself. Manners were very important to the English Mastiff and he did teach me a few things. So, here goes: My proper name is John O. Barleycorn. Big Guy gave me that name. AT YOUR SERVICE. And you can call me "Barley" – everyone else does.

Back to my story. We spent the first couple of weeks bonding, taking walks all around town, meeting people (sooo many people). Big Guy told me one day very soon we would be moving. I'm not a big fan of change and so you can see how I might get a little nervous. Big Guy assured me though, that I was going to be a much happier dog.

When we completed our move to the new home, and I could see what was around me, I was surely a lucky dog. Big Guy had been right. It was the happiest day of my life. There was so much land to run around on, so many wonderful smells. And we had seven more dogs too. I was part of a real working pack just as we are all intended to be.

The first thing to do was get to know the new pack. There was a lead dog named Windy who was the old man of the pack and the first trail dog of the company. Then there was; Sandy (a dog my size); Missy, the bear dog, Louie, the guard dog; and Sherman, Max and Fritz. Louie was called the guard dog because of his habit of sleeping with the horses by the picket line at night.

Another part of the new life was walking around and working with the saddle horses and pack animals who were both horses and sometimes mules.

The riding stock were Jemmy, Cowboy, Blackjack, Cheyenne, Gracie, Smokey, Tennessee, Jeb, and Rocket. The pack animals were Ester, Caveman, Ginger, Dawn, Lucy, Blondie, Festus, Bella, Freebie, Twister and Salty.

I had so many new friends. Just getting to know all of them and learning their names kept me pretty busy. Some were very interesting to know and some didn't seem too interested in making friends or visiting. Just like Tall Folks.

At first I thought they were big dogs, not horses. Well, I was young and didn't know. I just figured it out pretty soon. Their whole way of thinking is different from mine. One thing we do seem to have in common is apparently wanting to please Tall Folks. But horses get treated different. When we do something good or bad, we get told "good boy" or "bad dog" and patted or tousled and sometimes even given a treat, but horses are just expected to do right without reward. Seems sort of sad.

I was talking with one of the mules one day and he agreed it was sad. He said "Tall Folks just take equines for granted. That is probably because we have been around for so long." He also pointed out that horses enjoyed a higher status rating than pack stock. Horses were usually ridden and the mules, (even some other horses) carry the packs of supplies. Also, some equines, animals of the horse family, have more self respect for themselves. I had never really thought about that, but it seems to be right. I have always considered Salty to be a very smart mule.

Well, to continue my story, I had to learn how to act properly on the trail. There is a lot more to it than meets the eye. I learned not to go off chasing the smell of every stray skunk or coyote, not to chase rabbits or birds, to stay with the outfit and not wander off away from the trail. I also had to learn not to bark without a very good reason, and especially not at the other animals. I learned to walk with the horses and mules without getting stepped on or kicked. Let me tell you, a mule can kick!! Hard!! In any direction and fast. Sadly, Festus taught me that lesson the hard way.

And I learned to work with the Outfitter, Big Guy, and the other dogs too. I learned that our job was to stay with the pack outfit and act as "advanced re-con" for protection. (That is a fancy name I heard from one of the Clients on a trip once.) Sort of guard dogs, you understand. The job was to warn Big Guy and the other Tall Folks if there was a lion or wolf, or maybe a bear nearby.

You heard me right. Lions and wolves and bears were pretty common. We were a good pack and did our jobs well, so we didn't ever have anyone hurt by a bear or wolf or lion. We did, however, have a few instances on the trail from time to time.

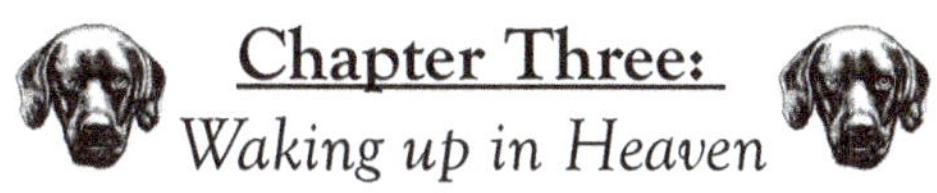

# Chapter Three:
## *Waking up in Heaven*

It was in the middle of winter when I went to live with Big Guy on the new place and we spent lots of time working on gear and tools for the trail repairs and pack trips, taking care of the other animals, and making plans. I didn't really have much to do with making plans though.

It seems that the business went like this: first we had to go out and work on the trails and repair them from the damage caused by weather during the winter. We would take the saws and shovels and axes out on the pack animals, make a camp for headquarters, and work out of that camp to the trails that we would be fixing. We would cut up limbs and logs that had fallen across the trails, dig up weeds and other things that had started to grow in the way and repair the actual trails when necessary by shoveling away problems or putting rocks in washouts. Big Guy explained all this to me as he worked, but I didn't really understand all I was learning. It is really hard to understand things you have never seen for yourself.

Then the Clients would come. Strange vehicles coming up the road; trailers hooked to pickups, equines loaded into trailers, gear and saddles in the back of the trucks. Those were the signs that we were getting ready to go into the Wilderness. I liked riding in the front of the truck best. The bed did scare me a little sometimes. Going into the Wilderness makes a dog's tail wag just thinking about it, even now.

The Clients were Tall Folks who would go into the Wilderness for various reasons. The Outfitter, and Big Guy, who was the wrangler and camp cook, would take them and their gear and let them ride some of the saddle horses (if they didn't have their own) and guide them to a camping location. It is easy to get lost in there if you don't know your way around. The Outfitter and Big Guy would provide tents, tables and seats if necessary, food and transportation in and out. Creel Canyon Outfitters was responsible for all aspects of the trip, in and out and while we were there, including the enjoyment and safety of the Clients and ourselves.

Clients came for several reasons. Mostly to hunt for elk, deer and sometimes bears. They also came to fish, take pictures and just for the experience of being there. Sometimes whole families came together.

Finally the weather got to be warm enough and clear enough for us to go into the Wilderness. I was pretty excited because this was my first trip. Some of the older dogs in the pack seemed to be taking it all in stride since they were old hands at it, but they, too, admitted that it was a big deal.

We arrived at the trail head and unloaded from the pickups and trailers. All the tools were ready, the pack animals loaded, the saddle horses ready and Big Guy got on his horse. That was my cue to fall in beside him and we were off.

It was a little later than they had planned when we finally were on the move. When we got to the meadow at Canyon Creek, it was nearly dark and we were all tired. Big Guy set up the tent, fixed something for them to eat, and fed me. That food seemed to taste better out here. I was liking this already. When we were through eating and the chores were done, we went to bed. I crawled into Big Guys sleeping bag and was sound asleep right away.

I woke up in the morning to the sounds of birds, and voices, and the gurgle of water from the river. And the most wonderful smell in the world. Thousands of pine trees giving off pure oxygen, wild flowers bursting out to greet spring, the special smell of free running water and all that wrapped up with thousands of acres of freedom. Okay, maybe freedom doesn't smell, but it was there anyway. Right outside the door of that tent.

I launched myself out that door, across the river which was a little brisk that early, and into the meadow full of wild flowers and around the big pine tree and over the piled up rocks. I made a big loop, ears flying, tongue hanging out, feet going as fast as I could make them. I ran back to camp, right up to Big Guy, and with my tail wagging as fast as it could, I shook off as much of the river as was left. So Big Guy could share, of course. He didn't seem to be too excited about sharing and I guess that was because he had done all this before. And he didn't seem to like the water either. But I did

I spent the rest of that day enjoying my first experience with being in the Wilderness. Big Guy and the Outfitter spent the day working around camp and getting all the tools ready, and setting up for the next day. I spent my time just enjoying the feeling of waking up in haven.

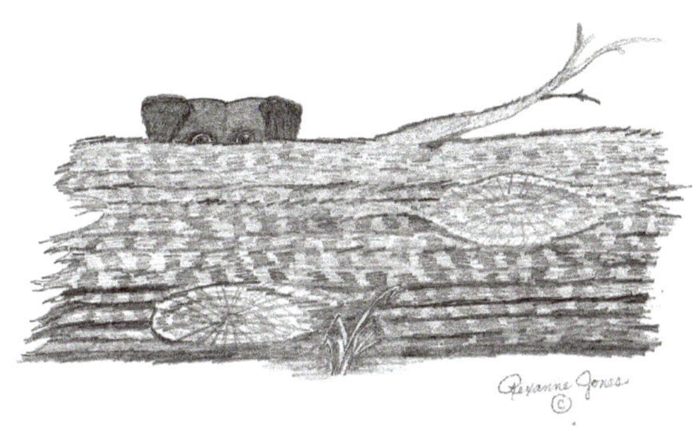

## Chapter Four:
*Barley Meets a Bear*

My first bear (that's how Tall Folks tell bear tales) was pretty scary because this was one of those times when I should have listened to Big Guy, but no, I was young and so smart. I thought I knew it all. We were on a day ride with two groups. We camped in the Blue Range Primitive Area, at Ribbon Tank, which is nestled in the foothills of the White Rocks Mountains, very close to the East side of Arizona, and got ready for our part of the ride. Big Guy and I were to go down river to Winter Cabin. The Outfitter, (the tall person who took care of the paper stuff and talked on his phone when it worked) was taking the bigger group to the Blue River.

As we started off, I decided that the other group was probably going to have more fun. I had been to Winter Cabin before but never over to the Blue River. I sort of eased up to the front and Big Guy called me back. I hesitated and ran back and forth and each time I could hear the other outfit getting further off. Finally, I just left my post and ran as hard as I could toward the sounds coming from the other outfit. I knew I had made a mistake right away because in very short order, I was lost. I continued on in the same direction, but not nearly as fast. Pretty soon I came around a little bushy bend in the river and right there in front of me was the

11

biggest bear I could ever imagine. I would say that he was the biggest bear I have ever seen, but I haven't really seen all that many bears.

Now, I came to a very sudden stop and stood very still. I looked around and was painfully aware that Big Guy was not anywhere near. Why didn't I listen to him? But no, I had to think for myself.

The bear was huge, even taller than Big Guy, when he stood up. And I could tell that the bear knew that I was there so I slowly crawled under a downed tree trunk with a lot of decaying bark and vegetation which I hoped would help hide my smell. The bear was obviously hungry as he was tearing into the rotting log where he was standing and grabbing paws full of grubs, a favorite diet for bears. But, there was more to that log than met the eye. Along with the grubs, there was a nest of hornets too. They did not like having their home disrupted by Mr. Bear. And Mr. Bear did not like getting stung all over either. The bear backed away, still being chased by the hornets. Night time was coming on fast and one by one the hornets quit the bear and were returning to their nest. But the bear was still there and still hungry. And I was still there too. But I resolved to fix that right away. While the bear's mind was still on the hornets, I decided to leave, fast. I turned around and headed back the way I believed I had come with my mind set on finding Big Guy as quick as I could. I had never missed him so much. After a short time that seemed like all night, I made it back to camp. There were the pack animals and saddle horses, the other dogs, the Clients, the bedrolls and tent, the warm fire and most important……Big Guy.

I was worried that I would be in big trouble with Big Guy and he would be mad at me, maybe even quit liking me. But he was glad to see me and just told me how worried he had been about my safety. I promised myself that from then on I would stay with the outfit and obey Big Guy when he called me and keep close so we could both be safe.

The Ranger, who looks after the Wilderness and teaches people how to take good care of the forests, was visiting our camp that night. He and

Big Guy talked about how it was the same for dogs and people alike. Everyone should stick together when in the forest, never go off without letting someone know where you are going to be and when you should be expected back. And be prepared for all emergencies as much as possible. And think ahead. Good advice, even for dogs.

## Chapter Five:
### *It' Not About How Tall You Stand.......*

One day, we were taking a group of Clients on an overnight trip which was going to be along the Middle Fork of the Gila River, and they had plans to try some fishing while there. The weather was extra nice, a little warm after some really cold nights and all the pack was feeling pretty frisky. The early spring smells were everywhere and even the horses and mules seemed to feel it.

We were all running back and forth and yipping a little bit with excitement, and telling each other big yarns about how important we were. I told them that I had grown very tall during the winter and how much taller I was now. The other dogs also had opinions about how much they had grown up and how much talker we all were now. We decided that tall was a very important thing and we certainly had a handle on it.

We made camp and Big Guy started setting things up. Horses were tethered, tent stakes were driven and the tent was ready. Fire wood was gathered and stacked and ready. Bed rolls and gear were unloaded from the pack saddles and ready to be used. And all the while, all of us in the pack were strutting around enjoying how big we had gotten over the winter. I stood up next to the front leg of one of the saddle horses, (you want to avoid doing that with a mule) and remarked that I now reached almost to her knee. Gracie seemed unimpressed.

It was almost dark, just as the sun was going down, when we spotted some visitors to camp. Just on the edge of the camp area, coming from the direction of the river, was a family of skunks…..Mom and two youngsters. Our whole pack was immediately on solid alert. Big Guy yelled at me to leave them alone. But I was so tall now and so important. The whole pack, as one, ran to confront the skunk family, with me in the lead. I did mention that I was very tall now, right?

As we approached the little family, we could hear them talking among themselves. (Yes, animals talk to each other.) The children were very worried about all these mean looking (and tall) dogs running up to them. The dogs did not seem friendly at all. "What are we going to do, Mother?" they said. In a very calm voice, the mother said "We are going to bow our heads and spray, children." And they did just that.

I had never been sprayed by a skunk before, nor had I been around someone who had. I can tell you right now, I hope to never be sprayed again. It was awful. Right in the face and eyes, a smell you can't wipe off, or get away from. And it don't wear off very soon either. Also, Big Guy and all the other Tall Folks wouldn't let us anywhere near them. The horses didn't even like us. Forget slipping into a bedroll in the middle of the night to keep warm. Those three short skunks had managed to spray every tall dog in the pack, and some of us who were slow, twice. It just goes to show you, it don't matter how tall you are, but what you can do with what you were given to work with that counts.

When anyone, person or dog, is out in the forest, a really good thing to remember is to leave things and folks alone when you don't know about them. In most cases, if you don't bother them, they won't bother you. And they live in the forest and are prepared and equipped to take care of themselves. You are the visitor.

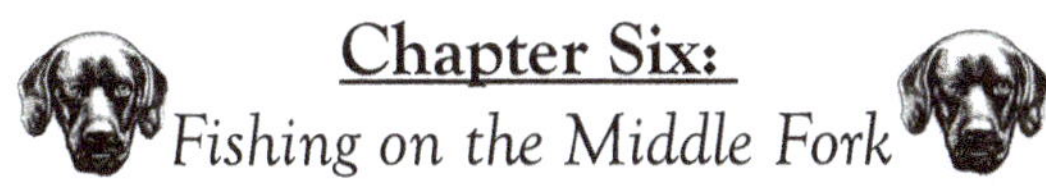

## Chapter Six:
### *Fishing on the Middle Fork*

I remember one interesting trip to the Middle Fork of the Gila River in particular, which was a lot more fun that meeting up with a skunk family. We had three clients from up North, around Albuquerque, (wherever that is) who were doctors Big Guy said. They brought their own horses for this trip and were here to catch some fish. They didn't bring any guns, which is good because it was not the season or time of year for hunting deer or elk or anything. But the fish should be biting pretty good. The days were warm but not too hot and the nights were still pretty cool. The water was cold and running swift still from the spring thaw. And the bugs were abundantly available. Fish really do seem to love bugs. It seems that the Middle Fork was known for its' supply of trout, a favorite of fishermen to catch and to eat.

When the Clients would catch a mess of trout, Big Guy would clean them and cook them over the camp fire. Most everyone really did enjoy those fish. And we in the pack got to eat the skins and tails. We didn't eat the bones because they could choke us;. And being dogs, we would have gulped them right down without thought about how they could be bad for us. (One more time when Big Guy was there taking care of me and keeping me in good shape.)

As usual, we made camp, unsaddled and unpacked the animals, and picketed them, set up the tent and Big Guy fixed some supper. It was getting a little late since we had spent the better part of the day on the ride into this area. He had allowed for just this event and had packed some steaks to cook on the campfire, along with potatoes and corn on the cob. (Big Guy is considered a really good cook and since I eat his food all the time, I would have to agree with that.)

After we had eaten, one of the Clients decided to try his luck at fishing. It was pretty late already and very soon he decided to give it up for the night without catching anything. I was pretty tired and ready for the bed roll myself.

I had never been on a "fishing" trip before. Dogs were not allowed on the actual hunts for elk and deer and bears, by law. (That was the rules set out by the Ranger and the Government, which is the really big boss.) I didn't really know what to expect, except that I had eaten trout before and really did like it. I was looking forward to that part myself.

The next morning, I woke up really early, just as the sun was coming up. But I was not the first one up. Oh, no. Seems fishermen don't sleep in at all and can't wait to get to the water. Big Guy was working on the fire and had coffee going. He had some eggs ready to put in the skillet and the potatoes were frying. When I walked over to him to say "good morning", he said that breakfast would be a little later, because the Clients were fishing and he was planning to cook some trout for breakfast. Sounded good to me.

I decided to wander down by the river and watch to see what "fishing" was all about. Like I said, this was my first fishing trip.

All three Clients were standing in the river, wearing little hats with things stuck in them, and chest high rubber boots with suspenders. And they were really working at catching something. Each one had a long pole called a "rod" and was whipping the line attached to it back and forth over the water. And it was doing some good too, I could see. Up and down the river, trout were jumping out of the water. And ever so often, one would get stuck on the end of the line attached to the pole and the Client would pull him in and put him into a basket he carried on a strap around his neck. All in all, I was pretty impressed with the way they could crack those "whips" and get those trout to jump up and get caught. And by now I was really looking forward to breakfast.

When the Clients had caught their "limit" of fish for the day, they came back to camp and Big Guy fried up the trout for all of us to eat. That was some really good meal. I got some meat from those fish too and it was really tasty.

The Clients stayed camped on the Middle Fork for three days, and each day was pretty much a copy of the first day. After breakfast that first day when we ate fried trout, they cleaned most of the fish and packed them in ice in a chest to take home. The weather was still pretty brisk and the fish would keep in the ice.

On the fourth day, we broke camp, packed everything up, including the ice chests with the fish, and were ready to go. It was still morning but it would be a long ride back home.

Just as we were about to leave, a small bear, a young one, came across up river from our camp. The trout were jumping a little, (after bugs in the air, it turns out,) and he was trying to catch a fish in his mouth. After a couple of tries, he was successful and caught a trout in his mouth and went off a little ways to eat his catch.

I just couldn't help myself. I had to try it. I ran to the river, waded right in and chased one of those trout jumping around. First, I got water up my nose. The second try, I slipped on the rocks below the water and went completely under. A guy could starve like this. On the third try, I caught one. I don't know who was more surprised, me or the fish. I immediately realized that I really didn't have a plan or know what to do with that fish now that I had him. He was slapping me in the face and ear with his tail and wiggling around and was all slickery and slimy in my mouth. And he didn't taste like the fish Big Guy had given me last night at all. I decided that I really didn't like raw fish. I didn't waste any more time. I spit him out. Right back into the river. I have since heard Clients on fishing trips call this "catch and release" and they do it a lot. It leaves the fish for the next guy to catch and ensures that there will always be fish available in the Middle Fork of the Gila River for the next people who come along to catch.

Maybe someday, you will get a chance to bring your camera and your fishing rod and come to the Wilderness to catch trout. I hope so. I know you will love it, but don't eat them raw.

## Chapter Seven:
### *Porcupine Quills*

It was getting along towards fall and we had two Clients making a trip into Cub Creek. They were a couple of very nice young ladies who were making the trip to take pictures and write a story. They were really friendly and treated me and all the pack with affection and respect. We could always get a pat or a rub behind the ear. I had my picture taken several times. It's always nice to be appreciated and, after all, us authors kind of have a lot in common and have to stick together. Of course, I wasn't an author just yet, but the idea did come to me during that particular trip.

We made camp and Big Guy and the Outfitter each went with one of the girls to explore and to find the best places to take pictures. That can be really hard in the Wilderness since everywhere you can look is beautiful.

Of course, I went with Big Guy. I have always loved to go and see all there is to see and smell all there is to smell and don't ever want to miss anything. Sometimes, I go with the Outfitter for that reason, but today I was going with Big Guy. We headed up stream and the other girl went with the Outfitter downstream. It was a beautiful day. Of course, most days in the Wilderness were beautiful if the weather was nice. Today, the weather was very nice.

Our pack was all around and some went with the Outfitter and the other girl and some went with Big Guy and myself. Max, Fritz and Louie went with us. And an old dog, who didn't always come along, named Chili, was along with us too. Chili was a grumpy dog, always, grumbling down in his throat about something or the other, which is probably why he got left at home a lot. Everything seemed to aggravate him. The sun was too hot or not warm enough, the water was too cold or too wet, his feet hurt, another dog was not doing what he thought they should be doing, and so on. We all just tried to ignore him and let him complain to himself. After all, he was apparently the oldest dog in the pack and had been coming to the Wilderness for several years. He should be entitled to some respect don't you think?

After several hours, we had taken lots of pictures and were about ready to head back to camp. The sun was low and it was beginning to get just a little chill in the air. We didn't really have to follow a trail here and the pack dogs with us were spread out around the riders. Chili was in the rear, coming along slow as he could and not get left behind. And, as usual grumping along the way. "Not much excitement here," he said as he lumbered along. And then, "Haven't seen any new things at all." And "I'll be glad when we get back to camp and I can rest." I thought I could surely understand why he got left at home a lot. But, of course, Tall Folks could not hear or understand him.

Just about a mile from our camp, an animal crossed our path. It was a big, full grown porcupine. For those of you who don't know, this fat guy is completely covered with spikes called quills which he can shoot at anything that seems to threaten him. And since they are big cowards, most everything and everyone threatens them. I had run into one before and for once I listened to Big Guy and left him alone. Sherman, one of the other dogs, did get a few quills in his nose and the Outfitter had to pull them out with a pair of pliers. Sherman told me how bad that hurt and I sure didn't want to be hurt like that so I was going to leave him alone now.

Just then a strange thing happened. Chili came running up from the back of the pack, and right at Mr. Porcupine. Big Guy yelled at him but no luck. He didn't even slow down. It turned out that one of the things about Chili that caused him to be left behind was that he hated porcupines. He had been really hit with quills when he was a pup and from them on he hated them and could not leave them alone. The Outfitter had had to pull quills out of him several times before.

Now Chili confronted that porcupine, who immediately raised his quills to strike and faced Chili ready to defend himself. Chili was barking wildly. Chili just kept on looking for a place to bite that porcupine. There just wasn't one since Mr. Porcupine was covered from one end to the other with those quills. I felt sorry for Chili and decided to run up there with him to try to help him. Maybe he would listen to me. Bad idea. As soon as that porcupine saw me, he decided that he was in fact under attack and fired his quills. Since Chili was in front of me, he got most of the quills right in the face and neck. Those quills were in his mouth, nose, ears, around his eyes and all down his neck. Because he had his mouth open to bite, the quills were all inside his mouth and in his tongue. And I got some too. Not too many, just in my nose, but they really did hurt.

Big Guy rode up then and run the porcupine away and gathered Chili up to take him back to camp and take care of the quill problem. He put Chili across his saddle and carried him on his horse back to camp. For once, Chili kept his mouth shut. It was full of quills and I think it hurt a lot for him to open it.

I got scolded for running up there and getting quilled myself, but in a gentle way because I know that Big Guy only cared about me and didn't want me hurt. And as a reminder to always leave porcupines alone. They have a way of winning.

When we got back to camp, the other girl and the Outfitter were already back. The Outfitter could see what happened to Chili and said that this would be the last time he came to the Wilderness because of his thing with porcupines. I sure didn't want to have any doings with them any more and I certainly didn't want to have to stay home because of quills.

Big Guy and the Outfitter put Chili down by the fire so they could see and the Outfitter got some Kerosene to put on the quills. They cut the ends of the quills off so the barb would let go and put the Kerosene on them to make them a little bit easier to pull and pulled all those quills out with a pair of piers. It took a long time and was really a job because Chili didn't want to be still and kept trying to bite and wriggle loose. If left in the skin, those quills would fester and each one would make a bad sore, which could become infected. It was a very serious thing.

For myself, I only had a few. I sat down in front of Big Guy, and let him pull them out. I bit my tongue a little bit when it hurt the worst but I didn't move and I didn't try to bite either. This was all my fault in the first place. When it was all done, Big Guy said he only had to pull nine quills. There was something like a hundred in Chili and getting them all out took late into the night.

We rode out the next day. I was really glad to be home. The places on my nose were still a little tender and I laid around for a while recovering from all that. Chili never went with us again.

All the animals and birds and other beings that live in the forest are made with ways and means to protect themselves and to eat and live in that environment and they know what to do to take care of themselves. The best thing that a person or a dog can do is to leave them alone. It is wonderful to just watch and enjoy the wildlife without disrupting them. They are an important part of the entire experience of seeing and enjoying the Wilderness.

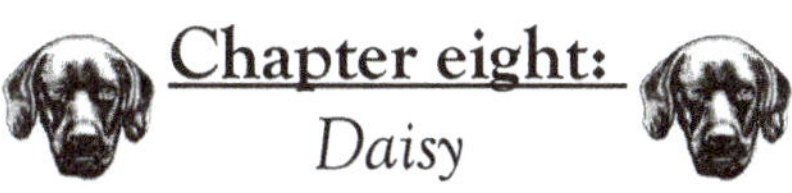

## <u>Chapter eight:</u>
### *Daisy*

We didn't have a Client after the porcupine incident for a couple of weeks. Big Guy went through all the gear and made any repairs that seemed to be needed, like the leathers on a saddle or the cinch on a pack saddle or the lead ropes and bridles and halters to be sure they were in good working order.

Then he made a trip into the big town, called Silver City, to get some things for the next trip that were not available around home. He bought groceries, mostly canned and dry goods, and Kerosene and coffee and flour and shortening and such. He would be gone all day and I resolved to make the best of that. I would get up on the couch that was on the porch and take the world's longest nap. For my nose, you know. I would still be available to assist and direct Big Guy when he got home and was putting all the things he had bought and brought home away. In the meantime, I was going to get that nap.

It was almost hard dark when I heard the truck coming and saw the headlights shine across the road that signaled that Big Guy was home. I got off of the couch and stretched hard, first my front half and then my back half. That always feels so good. Then I headed out to the driveway to meet Big Guy.

What a surprise I was in for! \

Seems that on his way home, Big Guy had stopped by the Alma Store and took care of some errands there. While he was there, he was given something to bring home with him!

Big Guy was getting out of the truck and he had a DOG in his arms. I didn't know what to think. Up until now, it had been just the two of us and now here was another dog. What would it be like? You remember that I am not a big fan of changes.

Big Guy set the dog down and I could see in the dim light that the new animal was short and stocky and had long ears and short legs and a long body. And it was a GIRL!

I could see that she had a nice face with big, pretty brown eyes and a cute nose. And she smiled at me. Okay, then, this might work. But she would have to understand that I was still the boss. At least that was what I thought when I first met Daisy. I really didn't know her very well then.

Daisy has a mind of her own and we are best friends now, but it took a while for me to realize that we are a team and I'm not the boss. I love going into the Wilderness and pack trips with Big Guy, and still love all the smells and such. But I am older now and I am content to keep the couch on the porch company more and more each day.

Not Daisy. That hound (her mother was a Red Bone Hound) loves to travel more than any dog I have ever met. Even here at home, she will take off and be gone all day. Sometimes she is gone for several days. She has friends all over the place and tries to visit all of them on a regular basis. I think she gets a snack at most of her friends' places too. Big Guy is always getting calls on his phone from someone who tells him that Daisy is at their house or business. Sometimes he has to go and get her but most of the time she comes home when she is ready. That is one traveling girl for sure. Everyone around here knows her and her name. She would not be happy in town or where she was kept in a yard. We are both very lucky to have Big Guy and live where we do.

When we were still working, before I retired, Daisy went with us taking Chili's place, I think, and we really did enjoy those trips. I knew that Big Guy was always there for me and that Daisy had my back. Nothing tops friends and family.

## **Chapter Nine:**

### *Another Way to Un-pack a Mule.*

There is a lot to Outfitting. Each animal is different and has needs that are different. Some are content to do the work they are doing and some have to be encouraged regularly to keep on working.

The saddles and pack saddles have to be comfortable and in good repair. They need to be fastened to the animal they are on in a very secure manner so that they don't slip. They need to meet the needs of the person depending on them. If it is a saddle horse, the saddle should not slip or slide on the horses' backs, and the rider and the horse should feel comfortable and also safe and secure. With the pack animals, it is very important to get their packs balanced and securely tied down so the mules and horses can move and travel comfortably and know where that pack is going to be so they can manage it and allow for changes in the landscape of the trails. Since the trails go up and down and around and over in all directions, the pack animals, especially, have to be able to manage their loads. Packing a mule is a real talent. Unpacking one is just as important….unless they unpack it themselves, which has happened at least once that I know of.

We were taking a pack outfit into Franz Springs and the trail was really tough. We had done a lot of work on it, but there were places where the trail was very narrow and wound around the front of a bluff with a long, steep drop down into a canyon on the outside.

Our mules and pack horses were some of the best. Steady, sure footed and dependable. We were very proud of the whole crew, dogs and horses and mules as well. And Big Guy and the Outfitter were really good at what they did too. Those packs were solid and right. No slipping there.

But things happen. This was going to be one of those times.

The Outfitter was in the lead, followed by two of the three Clients, then some of the pack outfit, Lucy, Blondie and Ginger, were next. The third Client was behind those three, followed by Festus and Twister in the back. Big Guy was bringing up the rear, keeping an eye on the animals in front of us. I was right behind Big Guy's horse, since that trail was really narrow and we were all in single file.

This was Daisy's first trip and she was right beside me. I was determined to teach her all that I had learned. She was having a really good time smelling and sniffing and just experiencing all the wonders around her,.

It was a warm afternoon and we had been trailing all day, with just a short stop for some sandwiches at lunch. I think we were all just a little bit relaxed and the riders were sitting easy on their horses. The pack animals were plodding along with their ears flopping and some even seemed to be napping while they walked. All in all, we were pretty relaxed and at ease.

And then all heck broke loose.

Twister, the last mule in the line came un-corked. He snorted, dropped his head, laid back his ears and began to buck as hard as he could. They didn't call him "Twister" for nothing and he was certainly cranking the jumps out, braying with each landing. Right where we were was the worst part of that bad trail and no one could tell what was going on.

Then things got worse fast. That mule was bucking all over that narrow trail and was in danger of falling off the side into the canyon. The other horses and mules were getting into the fray also. If they weren't actually bucking, they were jumping around and snorting and rearing up and acting up in general. All the riders had their hands full with their mounts.

Right beside the trail, where all those animals and people had just passed by, was a huge rattlesnake. Apparently he was sleeping in the sun and was not noticed by the animals, including the dogs, who were supposed to be watching for just such a thing. And the snake had not noticed us either.

Rattlesnakes have a very strong odorl. In almost all cases, the horses and the dogs would have smelled him. He had just shed his skin and that might have suppressed his smell somewhat. Also, rattlesnakes are very sensitive to vibrations in the ground around them and can smell pretty good themselves. How everyone, pack outfit, dogs and snake included managed to miss each other is a mystery. But it happened.

Just as Twister got even with him, the rattlesnake woke up, coiled and began to rattle. I guess the snake woke old Twister up and scared the fool out of him.

Twister continued to crank and buck and the pack saddle began to slip. The britchin', the strap around his rump which was there to keep the saddle from slipping forward when going downhill, came loose and allowed the saddle to slide up on Twister's neck some. By this time, the canvas that covered the packs was loose and flapping around, the mule was braying and bucking, and all the stuff that had been in his pack was flying around and falling down into that canyon. All this seemed to me to take place in slow motion.

The Outfitter was in the lead and couldn't really tell what was happening behind him. He could just see all the commotion. Big Guy got off his horse and threw some rocks at the rattlesnake, which made him crawl back into the rocks behind him and away from the trail. Good thing too, because none of the animals were going to settle down until he was gone.

Finally, Twister did settle down and quit bucking. Just a little hop now and then because the canvas was still there and the pack saddle had slipped down and was now hanging along his ribs on one side.

Big Guy walked along the pack train and calmed and talked to the animals and checked on the Clients, and the Outfitter came from the other end and was doing the same thing.

All the people were okay. None of the animals were injured. But, the stuff that had been in the packs was completely unloaded. A few things were scattered on the trail, but most of it was at the bottom of the canyon. The tent and beds were on the first two mules, and some of the food was okay. There was no way we were going to be able to get the stuff that was in the canyon. We squared up Twister, put his pack back together best we could and continued on to camp.

All in all, it had been a pretty exciting day for Daisy. She had enjoyed every bit of it too. She is one of the bravest dogs I have ever met and I am proud that we are friends.

When we got to camp, and everything was set up and ready for the night, the Tall Folks all talked about how they didn't have to unload one mule because Twister had done that for himself.

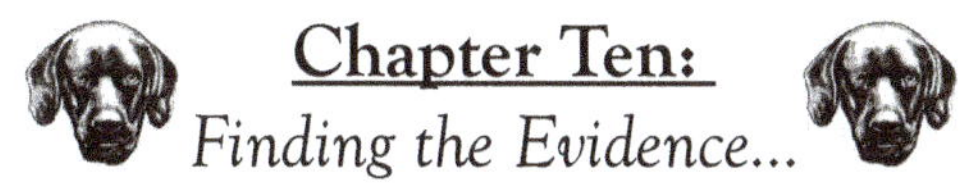

## <u>Chapter Ten:</u>
### *Finding the Evidence...*

On one trip we had just one Client, and he was going to be set up with a camp at Yamm Canyon for a week. The Outfitter and Big Guy would make camp, and then leave him there for the week and go back and pack him out. He would keep a saddle horse to ride, but the other animals would be coming out with Big Guy and the Outfitter. At the end of the week, when they went back into the Wilderness for the Client, they would take the pack outfit back in and bring him and his camp out.

Daisy and I went along together. She was getting to be a better trail dog all the time and I was really proud of her. It didn't hurt that she was a hound and had such a wonderful nose for smells. And she was smart too. I had learned that this girl didn't need a boss.

While the Outfitter and Big Guy unpacked the mules, set up the tent and got all the camp things done, Daisy and I decided to take a little walk around the area and see what was going on in the neighborhood so to speak. We headed out a little uphill for a ways and then found a trail to follow. It was a little strange because it seemed to be a cow trail. There were not usually any cattle, (bovines) in the Wilderness but that was what it seemed like anyway. It wandered around the face of the hillside instead of up and down more like a deer would make. And it smelled like a cow. I knew that was right because you could trust Daisy's nose all the time.

After we had gone a ways and were out of sight and sound of the campsite, we came into a small meadow, filled with lush green grass and in the center was a small water hole. It was a really pretty place and Daisy and I decided to sit down and rest and enjoy the view before going down there to get a drink of water.

Good thing we did. Just then a huge wild bull came out of the brush and headed for the water hole. He had probably been left behind by some rancher years ago and had managed to escape being caught and maybe even being seen for all those years. He had a spotted hide, no sign of a brand and exceptionally long and pointed horns. He was old and cagey and we could see that he would probably be mean if confronted. We had no plans to confront him that was for sure. We just sat there and kept our mouths shut and continued to watch.

When the bull was almost to the water hole, a huge bear came out of the woods opposite from where the bull had been. That is two huge animals for sure in the same place. And both were headed for the same water hole.

Sometimes animals in the wild will get along with each other and sometimes they are territorial and don't want anything or anyone else in their space. It was beginning to look like that was going to be the case here because the bear stood up on his hind legs and roared in the direction of the bull. The bull in turn dropped his head and bellowed. Both continued on their paths to the water hole.

For our part, Daisy and I sat very still and kept very quiet. We just watched.

When the bear and the bull got close to the water, they began to make lots of loud noise, and shake their heads and make threatening gestures at each other. We could tell from where we were that they were not intending to get along.

About that time, they lunged at each other. The bull was gouging at the bear with those horns and the bear was swiping at the bull with his long claws and biting the bull on the neck No friendship there.

Both animals were old and each was set in his own ways. This was going to be a fight to the death. Daisy suggested that we didn't need to stay for the ending so we got up and headed back to camp.

What we had witnessed was very exciting and we wanted to tell=Big Guy and the Outfitter what we had seen. I tried my best to get them to understand and Daisy even tried falling down and playing dead dog to get her point across. But Tall Folks just don't speak dog very often and I don't think they got it. Big Guy did say that he realized that something we considered to be very important had happened but he didn't know what.

Some good always comes out of almost everything and that was the case in this case. The next season, when we had occasion to bring some Clients back to this same campsite, Daisy and I wanted to show Big Guy what we had seen the year before. We danced around him and barked and yipped and finally, after supper when the chores were done, and it was still a little daylight, we got him to follow us.

We led him to the little meadow with the grass and water hole where we had seen the bear and bull fighting the year before. We all walked down to the water hole and there, beside the water, was the skull and a small piece of hide from that old bull. The bear had won.

Big Guy could see that it was a bovine animal and read the sign of the fight between the bear and the bull which was still in the mud by the water. At last he understood what we had been trying to tell him.

Daisy and I felt very close to Big Guy right then. It is always a good feeling when you can communicate with someone you care about and feel that they know and understand what you are telling them. That is very hard sometimes for dogs and people.

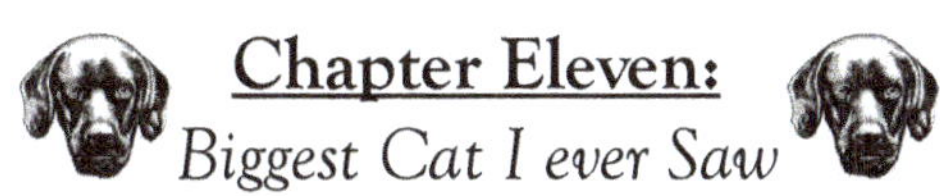

# Chapter Eleven:
## *Biggest Cat I ever Saw*

We had a couple of cats that stayed around the feed barn and caught mice and rats. There is not usually a lot of love lost between a cat and a dog. You've probably seen the cartoons. We did not have house cats. (I was glad. They smelled funny to me, and used the bathroom in the house….. Yuck.) Again, as I have said before, I left them alone and expected them to do the same for me. Consequently I didn't have much experience with the ins and outs of cats. I had never even talked to one. Furthermore, I had no immediate plans to begin either. I did mention that they smelled funny to me, right?

Well, this one time, we got a trip with three Clients who were lion hunters. They were going to set up a base camp and "run" lions with their dogs from there.

Seems that a lion or lions were killing cattle and the rancher wanted the hunters to chase the lions and get them to move further up in the mountains and away from their cattle.

When the hunters showed up, they had their own horses and their own pack of dogs. These dogs were very different from us. We had been taught to respect the wildlife and to mind our own business. These "lion" dogs were specifically purposed to chase and tree lions and to harass them into moving into another territory. These dogs did not run loose like we did. They did not have the freedom of the camp either. They were each on their own lead. A lot of times that lead was attached to the belt of a lion hunter. I felt kind of sorry for them since I enjoyed my freedom so much.

They were a stuck up bunch of dogs too. They made it quite clear right up front that they were above us and did not intend to be friends or to hang around with us in any way because they were there to work and do their jobs. Like we weren't????

I had never seen or smelled a mountain lion. Big Guy told me that a lion was a really big cat like the ones at the barn. I still didn't exactly understand what that meant.

The next day, the hunters got ready to "strike the trail" which meant that they were going to go out in the area where they thought the lion might be and crisscross back and forth with the dogs until they could get the scent of the lion and tell which direction it was headed in.

Big Guy and the Outfitter were going to stay with the camp and wait for the hunters to do their job. And wait for the lion dogs to do their jobs too.

The first day the hunters and their dogs went out fairly early and were gone all day. They came back close to dark and said that they had not had any luck finding the lion. They had seen some sign, (that's poop in other words) and the dogs had not been able to pick up the trail. It seems that there were a lot of rock in the area and that lion had been sticking to the rocks and not leaving any tracks and very little smell.

The second day, they did finally find a lion. It was a young lion, probably last years' cub which would make it a little over a year old. The sign showed that there were two lions in the group. The other one, older then the yearling, would more than likely be the mother lion. She was showing herself to be old and smart and experienced in being hunted because she was outsmarting the hunters and their dogs so far.

They did trail the young lion, but lost him in the rocks. The dogs were having a hard time staying on the scent.

On the third day, they were a little late leaving camp. I think they were getting discouraged by their lack of luck in "treeing" those lions.

When they had gone, Daisy and I decided to take a little trip of our own. We had been hanging pretty close to camp and were getting a little bored. At least Daisy was bored. I had been taking my full share of naps and didn't mind being bored.

We headed out, up canyon, and a little away from the rocks that the hunters and dogs were working in. Soon, Daisy dropped her nose down and put it just above the dirt under her. I could see that she was smelling something important and sniffed myself as well as I could. I don't have her nose. Sure enough, there was a little whiff of something vaguely familiar. I just couldn't quite place it but it was there. And Daisy had it placed all right. "CAT" she said. And she was right. Not exactly the smell from the barn but pretty close.

Just then, the craziest thing happened. Daisy raised her head, opened her mouth and out came the most beautiful baying sound I had ever heard. It was the sound a true hound makes when they are on the scent of a trail. Daisy had struck the trail of that lion and she was on it. Voice singing loud and clear like a harp she took off and followed the trail. I, of course, followed her. That bugle voice of hers' could be heard for miles and it raised "goose bumps" and the fur on my neck. I had never heard anything like it but I liked the sound. We were on the trail of a mountain lion!!!

Back at the camp, Big Guy and the Outfitter had heard Daisy sing too. Big Guy knew what that sound meant as soon as he heard it. He and the Outfitter both broke and run to the horses and saddled up. They were headed out to help Daisy. The Outfitter brought his gun in case he needed to use it.

Over in the rocks, the lion hunters and their dogs also heard Daisy's song. They also knew what that sound meant. Daisy, not their dogs, had found the trail and was in hot pursuit. They, too, gathered up their stuff and headed in the direction of the clear notes of Daisy's voice.

Daisy followed her nose and I followed Daisy. We were running flat out. Daisy's legs are pretty short so flat out was not as fast as I could run but we were still covering lots of ground. Every few steps she would raise her head and send that wonderful sound up to the sky. It was a beautiful thing to hear. I have no idea what the lion thought hearing that song but I know that she heard it too.

After a while, the ground began to change. We were getting higher and the trees were getting taller and closer together. A couple of times Daisy would stop and run in little circles to be sure she had the scent. The lion was trying every trick she knew to throw off the dogs. But it didn't work with Daisy. She would soon pick up the scent, raise her head and send out that wonderful bay and we were off again. I just followed her and watched her back. Not that she needed any help right now but she might when we caught up with that lion. And I was sure that we would catch the lion. I was not so sure what we were going to do with it then.

Daisy was having the time of her life. This was a long way from a giveaway dog in a cardboard box in front of the Alma Store. I was so proud for her, and of her.

We pushed through a tight fit of tall pines growing right next to each other and up a really steep bluff or sandstone rocks. It was a struggle for Daisy with her short legs, but she didn't even seem to notice. She just jumped right up there like she did this every day. I had a little struggle myself when it was my turn.

When we got to the top, we found some really big rocks with a twisted cedar tree growing right up in the middle of them. Up in one of the very top branches of that tree sat the mother lion.

That was my first time to see a lion. That was the biggest cat I have ever seen. And I could really smell it now and it did smell like the cats at the barn only much stronger. I didn't like the smell of the barn cats and I really didn't like the smell of this big cat either.

Daisy was still singing her song but with a different beat now. (Hunters call this "baying treed" I would learn later.) She was right under that lion, and jumping up at that tree. Sometimes, she would even climb up a little ways on some of the branches. The lion was hissing and growling back at her and would sometimes take a swipe in her direction with a paw full of claws. I barked a little for back up.

Okay, the lion was treed. Now what????

I could see that things could not stay the way they were right now for very long. Something would have to happen. And it did.

About that time, the "cavalry" arrived. Maybe not John Wayne but close. Big Guy and the Outfitter came up over that ledge and was I ever glad to see them. The Outfitter had his gun and fired several shots into the air right under that lion. She quit that tree in one big leap and headed for parts unknown at a high rate of speed. Just as she jumped, the lion hunters also showed up and added their guns to the shooting. That lion didn't even look back.

Daisy just sat there with a big smile on her face. She was one happy dog. She knew what she had done and so did the lion hunting dogs. From that day forward, they showed her the utmost respect. As for me, I will always remember the wonderful, chilling sound of her baying on the trail and "treed" at the end. And I have a lot of respect for her too.

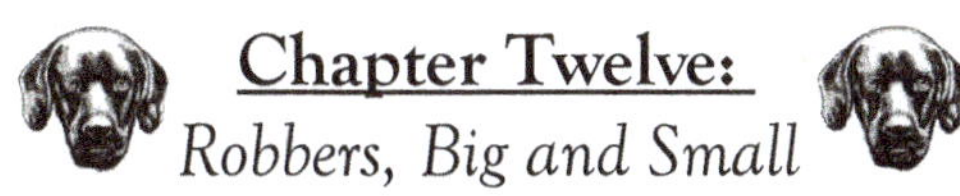

## Chapter Twelve:
### *Robbers, Big and Small*

On one trip, we had a family of Clients, a man and his wife, and three children. The kids were a little older and really having a good time riding horses and enjoying the sights and the country. There were two boys, Josh and Bob, and a girl named Janis. Josh was 12, Bob was 11 and Janis was 9. They were good ages to enjoy all that a trip like this has to offer. Just to be on the safe side, though, their parents had brought along some things for the kids to enjoy and be entertained with. They had books, some games and a small portable radio, which didn't usually work up here in the mountains, by they played with it anyway.

They weren't hunting or fishing, but instead, just camping and riding horses and taking pictures. It was a family outing and they were planning to stay camped for a week.

As usual we got to the campsite, unpacked and tethered the stock, and Big Guy set up the tents and fixed the camp.\We had our tents, the Dad and the boys had a tent and Mom and Janis shared a tent also.

There is a lot to do to set up a proper camp, and especially in the Wilderness. Because the country must be kept pristine and in the best possible condition, all effort must be made to do things right. For instance, no trash or refuse can be left about. All signs of the camp should be removed when you leave. There has to be special attention paid to the camp fire to be certain to avoid any possible chance of forest fire. Also, things must be attended to in order to make the camp more comfortable and safe. A good supply of wood is a must. And all food items must be put up in a safe manner to avoid animals coming into camp in search of food. Bears are especially apt to come looking if they smell food, but lots of other animals will come to the smell of food too. Skunks, and raccoons in particular are little camp robbers. Which brings us to the story of the kids in this little family.

Josh and Bob had brought several different items with them and each one was not inclined to share their items with the other one. Comic books, a rubic cube, and that radio were Josh's. A book about Treasurer Island, two puzzles and a yoyo belonged to Bob. Janis had her Barbie doll, and her favorite hair brush and two barrettes. Also, Dad had a pocket watch and Mom had a wrist watch and a silver trimmed comb that she kept on her bedroll in their tent. You could tell that these items were very important to their owners.

The first morning, Janis complained that the boys must be playing tricks on her because she couldn't find her hair brush. Her mom told her that she had probably left it somewhere and forgotten where and Mom combed Janis' hair with her comb and put the barrettes in. Mom asked the boys if they had seen the brush, but they said they had not.

That night Dad couldn't find his pocket watch. He looked and looked and asked everyone but no one had any idea where it had gotten off to. Now there was a mystery.

Over the course of the next few days, one comic book, the comb, both little puzzles, the rubic cube, and Mom's wrist watch all came up missing. There seemed to be a robber around camp but no one had seen anyone.

It was time for us guard dogs to get to work. People under our care were losing things and we were not catching the thief. I decided to stay up at night instead of crawling into Big Guy's bedroll to sleep. Daisy said she would help me and maybe we could solve the mystery.

Sure enough, along in the wee early morning hours, when we were getting really sleepy and wanting to go get into that bedroll, we finally spotted the robber.

A big raccoon came slipping along from tent to tent, and snatched the yoyo. But the sure give away was when he tried to get off with that little radio. He had been visiting camp every night but not for the food. Instead, he was after the loot.

I had seen pack rat nests and crows' nests full of stolen treasurers before but this was my first time to catch a raccoon in the act. Now, how were we going to fix this?

Daisy had a possible answer. We would follow the raccoon and see where he was taking the things he was stealing and maybe we could get them back. Daisy fell in on the raccoon's scent and we trailed him back to an old hollow log, and sure enough, there the stuff was. Now we had to get Big Guy to come and rescue it all. We could grab a couple of things but we sure didn't want to get caught with them and have the camp think we were taking them.

Back at camp, we barked and yipped and jumped around and ran back and forth to get some attention. It is really hard to communicate with Tall Folks when they don't understand what you want to tell them. Finally, Big Guy got the idea that we were telling him something and followed us to the log and the raccoon. At last the mystery was solved. Camp Robbers turned out to be a single raccoon with a sense of humor.

Later, back home, we had another Robber incident. Big Guy left the butter out on the counter in the kitchen. He usually puts everything away but this time he did not. If he put the butter in the refrigerator it would get hard and be difficult to spread.

When he got up, the end of the butter stick was missing. Paper and all. He decided that it had to be a mouse. He would fix that and put the butter into a dish with a cover so the mouse couldn't get to it.

The next morning, the Butter Mouse had struck again. He had moved the lid to the dish and eaten almost all of the end of the butter in the dish.

"Curse you, Butter Mouse!" Big Guy decided to set a trap for the mouse. He chose a nice trap, and of course, baited it with butter. What else? He sat it on the counter where the butter dish had been and went to bed.

The next morning, the first thing Big Guy did was to check his trap. Yep, Butter Mouse had been there all right. The butter was all licked away, but the trap was still set. "That's it! You're going down, Butter Mouse" and Big Guy decided right then and there that he would out smart that Butter Mouse. He went to the store and got a sticky trap. That is one that would stick to the feet of the mouse when he stepped on it. Big Guy baited it with butter, of course.

The next morning, first thing, he rushed to the kitchen and checked that trap. Surely that Butter Mouse would be in it, right? Nope. No butter. No mouse.

Butter Mouse: four; Big Guy: zero.

The answer turned out to be put the butter in the refrigerator It will be hard to spread, but it will be there and the Butter Mouse can't open the refrigerator door..

Whether it's hair brushes and portable radios or just butter, a Robber is a Robber, big or small.

As I told you, I'm retired now. Daisy makes her rounds. We don't go into the Wilderness any more. Big Guy keeps pretty close to home and stays busy. He is on the fire department, and an EMT on the ambulance. In addition, he takes care of the park and civic things around the area as well. He still cooks but now it is at a café close by. Our horses are retired too. We don't see the Outfitter and the other pack dogs at all. But Big Guy talks about wanting to get involved with the search and rescue group here.

Search and Rescue is a group of people, on foot, with vehicles and horseback, who go out to find people who are lost or in trouble. Since Big Guy has spent so much time in the Wilderness and knows this whole area so well, he will be able to do a lot to help out when someone is in need. He really likes to help people.

Daisy is interested in going with Big Guy on the searches for lost folks. I know that she would have a great time going into the mountains again and with her nose, she could really be a lot of help. I might even go some time. But she won't need a boss.

And to that end, there is a new dog in the family.

Skeeter is still a teenager and sometimes a meat head. Daisy and I are trying to teach him all we can. When he will listen, that is.

He comes from a really good family. His mother is blue lacey and his father is catalahoula and hanging tree. For those of you who don't know, that is royalty for cow dogs. And I am sure that he will work into a really good working dog when Big Guy and the others go out to rescue someone.

Well, it's getting near my nap time now. Guess we will visit another time. I am headed for that couch on the porch. The sun is warm there and I really do enjoy my naps. Stop by again and visit. Daisy and I will be glad to see you.

www.ingramcontent.com/pod-product-compliance
Lightning Source LLC
Chambersburg PA
CBHW050019040726
47599CB00014B/1456

*9781954368903*